To Omer, his sisters, and to his grandfather, Abbas
for all their help and support

JANETTA OTTER-BARRY BOOKS

*Omer's Favorite Place* copyright © Frances Lincoln Limited 2011
Text and photographs copyright © Ifeoma Onyefulu 2011
www.ifeomaonyefulu.co.uk

First published in Great Britain and in the USA in 2011 by
Frances Lincoln Children's Books, 4 Torriano Mews
Torriano Avenue, London NW5 2RZ
www.franceslincoln.com

A catalogue record for this book is available on request from the British Library

ISBN: 978-1-84780-241-5

Set in Green

Printed in Dongguan, Guangdong, China by Toppan Leefung in October 2010

1 3 5 7 9 8 6 4 2

# OMER'S
# FAVORITE
# PLACE

## Ifeoma Onyefulu

FRANCES LINCOLN
CHILDREN'S BOOKS

Hello, my name is Omer.

I like playing at home.

I'll tell you all the places
where I play, and you can guess
where my favorite place is.

I like playing in front of our house
but my big sister, Reem, always
wants to play *Korki* there.

And my sister Shirin
just wants to push
me in my car,

play hide and seek,
or climb the rubber tree.

I like playing near the front door,
but that's where Reem likes to sit
and make coffee for Mama.

I like playing in the living room, but everyone says, "Omer, you'll break the sofa!"

"Let's play *Gebeta* instead," says Reem.

So I play at the back of the house,
but sometimes our nanny, Lubaba,
needs my help.

I like playing in the garden, but sometimes Mama says, "Omer, please water the plants for me."

I like playing in the hallway but it's where Aunt Seida likes to sit and chat on the phone.

I like playing in a small room next to our house, but that's where Aynalem, our maid, prepares *Injera* meal.

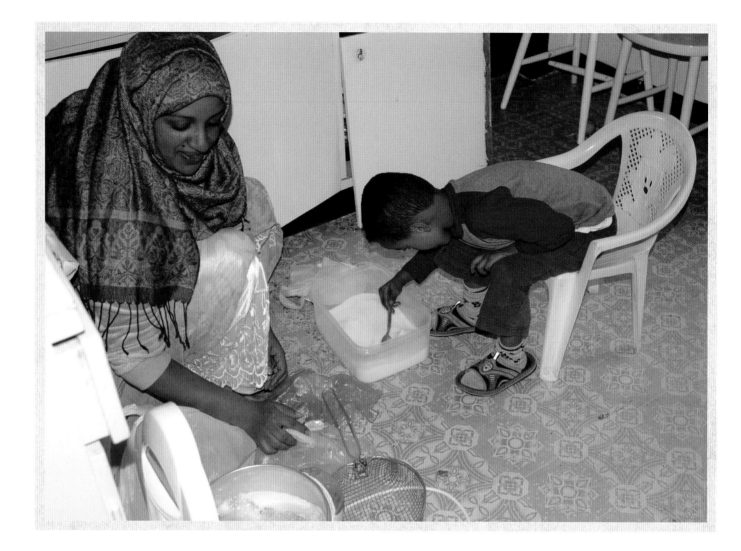

I like playing in the kitchen
but sometimes Mama needs me
to help her with the cooking.

I like playing on the dining table,
but I have to put away my toys.

I like playing in the store-room, but
I don't have enough space for my toys!

I like playing in my sisters' room,
but they always want to play *Atamata*.

Now I play behind the sofa,
where it is nice and quiet.

I can stay there all day,

looking at my book,

drawing a picture,

playing with my toys
or eating snacks!

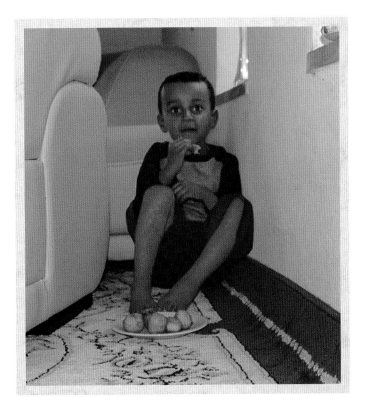

I say to Papa, "Can you guess where my favorite place is?"
But Papa doesn't know.

Can you guess?

It's behind the sofa!
That's my favorite place
of all!